HOW TO SUCCEED IN THE AGRICULTURAL AERIAL AVIATION BUSINESS

HOW TO SUCCEED IN THE AGRICULTURAL AERIAL AVIATION BUSINESS

RICK McCORD

PALMETTO
PUBLISHING
Charleston, SC
www.PalmettoPublishing.com

How To Succeed in The Agricultural Aerial Aviation Business

First Edition

Paperback ISBN: 979-8-8229-1858-0
eBook ISBN: 979-8-8229-1859-7

This book is dedicated to my wonderful and loving best friend, my wife, Laurie McCord, without whom I could have done nothing. Ten to twelve hours in a plane can really tax you beyond what your physical and mental mind seems to be able to handle, but God's grace and my wife's support have pulled me through it. There were times, more times than I wish, that I would come home completely wiped out and be in the most bearish mood possible. Laurie always accepted me, no matter what mood I was in or what idiotic things I said, knowing that it wasn't me but the product of me being mentally wiped out. I love you, sweetheart, and thanks for putting up with me for almost four decades.

■ ■ ■

Table of Contents

CHAPTER 1

Is It for Me?

There are a lot of young and upcoming pilots that look at ag pilots working fields with eyes of grandeur. I've heard so many times, "You have the job everyone dreams of" and "Is it as fun as it looks?" My response to the first question is, "It's very rewarding in some cases," and to the latter question, "It is for the first week of flying; then it becomes a job!"

The term *crop duster* that a lot of people still use when referring to those crazy cowboy pilots originated back in the early days of using airplanes as a tool. Applying insecticides in the form of dusts is where it comes from. Sulfur was being used as an insecticide in the form of a dust and was a very dangerous product as it was extremely flammable. In the earlier crop dusters, they actually placed rearview mirrors on the planes in case the dust was to ever ignite somehow. The pilot could then see the flame coming up behind them, shut their gate, and turn away so the trail of flames wouldn't catch up to them.

Most ag pilots I know like to be referred to as aerial applicators rather than the old term crop dusters. One of the first ag operations to come into existence was Delta Ag, which later became Delta Airlines.

I started working on my private pilot's license back in 1977 upon the request of my father, who ran a very successful business. He needed a pilot to carry him around to his different offices, so he paid my way toward my private license. I farmed also and had employed ag pilots to take care of my crops. As a lot of pilots do, I dreamed of becoming a professional ag pilot only to have my dad say, "No way!" It seemed every year we'd hear of an ag pilot either flying through a set of power lines or into the ground or trees, or just having plain engine failure. He'd see nothing of his son becoming one of these cowboys in the sky.

My father went home to be with the Lord in 1985. Then through a bunch of bad decisions in my early life, I found myself in bankruptcy, and it was time to grow up. Luck was on my side, and one of my father's best friends, Kenny Carlisle (a.k.a. Big Daddy), had a Cessna Ag Truck and had just lost his pilot due to a lost medical certificate. As a result, I got my first opportunity to climb into a spray plane.

Back in 1986 there weren't any two-seated ag planes, or at least any I knew of. I can remember like it was yesterday, as I'm sure most pilots remember the truly high points in their flying careers, the first day I climbed into this Ag Truck. I needed to act like this would be a walk in the park to my new boss, Big Daddy, as I was about to make this maiden flight, and I had to show him my professionalism—after all, I didn't want him to see how freaked out beyond belief I was. Prior to my flight, the plane had been moved to an airport to have some engine work by another pilot. The work had been completed, and it was time to fly it back home. I taxied out to the end of runway 18, and checking that everything looked OK, I placed both hands on my legs and tried to get them to quit nervously shaking. I pushed the throttle to full power, and I immediately almost ran off the left side of the runway.

I was not ready for the power and the torque this plane had versus the small planes I had flown prior to this. I couldn't believe it when it seemed like I rolled five feet and the plane leaped into the air. Big Daddy's strip was grass, as most rural ag strips are, and was close to two thousand feet long. I thought, *I've got to go somewhere and make some practice landings first where I know no one will be watching before making my virgin landing on the short strip*. I chose the Gideon, Missouri, airport, which was built by the government back in the World War II days as a crosswind airport. I thought, *Perfect, long and wide*. Well, that didn't seem to matter because as soon as my three wheels touched down pretty much at the same time, I discovered this plane had in its mind that it wanted to immediately leave the runway and become a grain sorghum harvester. I gave plenty of power to get it back on the runway and then tried again to stop my legs from shaking. It seemed like this plane and some of my body parts had thoughts of their own and were not listening to my wishes.

I took off again, circled to land, and almost ran off the runway a second time. It wasn't pretty, but I kept it on the runway this time. That was the extent of my training on takeoff and landing in this particular plane. I went on to my grass runway that I'd use for the next six years.

Over the years I've had some pretty good mentors who gave me tidbits of wisdom. Most pilots have heard the saying that "there are old pilots and bold pilots but not many old bold pilots." Then I had a competitor (a bad mentor) who had been working for several years and counted what fertilize load he was on by the beer cans in his floorboard. I didn't follow that latter practice, and it was just as well as this particular beer-and-whiskey-drinking pilot ended up totaling twenty-two aircraft during his career, including accidentally hitting his son in the head with his tire while he was flagging. Never did figure out how it didn't kill him. This pilot had to eventually quit as Lloyd's of London would no longer insure him, and they'll insure almost anyone.

Through this book I'm going to discuss various aircraft, the old and the new, as well as the following:

1. GPS systems and how they work, weather flying, and using the weather in ways your private pilot instructor warned you against.

2. Dry work versus liquid with different systems, including the topic that maybe should be the first consideration: SAFETY!

3. What it costs to get started and what kind of income you can expect.

4. Real-life experience that I have had and some stories of fellow ag pilots that I've known over my thirty-eight years of working in the ag aerial application industry.

5. Dealing with the FAA successfully and making them happy.

6. National and state associations that you should rely on and what they do for us; working in an environment and with the public where there are several looking for an easy lawsuit.

7. Mapping and job planning systems.

8. Dealing with your local USDA inspector and making them happy.

So is becoming an ag aerial applicator in your future? If you think it is, I hope this book gives you a little insight into the good and the bad and sometimes the ugly. This job is by far the most taxing job on the body and mind of any job I've ever had, but it can also be one of the most rewarding. I've known pilots that have made as much as $250,000 per year, and that's working maybe eight to ten months of the year. But be prepared: this will probably involve flying in the neighborhood of five or six hundred hours a year.

When things get tough, just remember the sort of comment I mentioned at the beginning of this chapter: "You have the coolest-looking job ever." That will bring you back to reality.

CHAPTER 2

Planes, Trains, and Automobiles

I tried thinking of a clever title for this chapter about the various planes, and this is all I could think of in discussing a variety of tools to accomplish the tasks at hand. Having a farming background, I think, has given me a better perspective on what our planes do and why they're called by their specific names. One of the first ag planes was the Snow (named after Leland Snow), who many consider to be one of the founding fathers of ag aviation. Other spray planes include the Cessna Ag Wagon, Cessna Ag Truck, and Ag Cat (which got its name from a World War II plane), as well as some planes produced by Thrush Aircraft Corporation. These planes are tools, just as a farm tractor is a tool for farmers. Our planes are not merely a means of traveling from point A to point B but rather give us a way to do a needed job for farmers that they can't do—and get it done in a very timely manner.

Most ground spray rigs sporting boom lengths from 90 to 120 feet and traveling approximately 14 miles per hour take twenty to thirty minutes to spray a forty-acre field, whereas we can spray the same one in five to seven minutes.

As I mentioned in the first chapter, I cut my teeth in a C-188 or Cessna Ag Truck, and it's powered by a Continental IO-520, 300 horsepower. It is equipped with wire cutters on the leading edge of the landing gear and a wire cutter that runs up the center of the windshield. It also has a cable that runs from the top of the cockpit to the top of the tail, which is used to prevent the tail from getting into electrical wires that spread all across this land. All models of Ag planes have this cable, at least all that I know of do. The Ag Truck has a 280-gallon hopper. This is a good plane to start, especially if you're buying it yourself, as you can find them fairly reasonable in costs compared to some of the larger aircraft. They have their limits, though, especially when working off a short runway, as they do love the real estate.

I went from an Ag Truck to an Air Tractor 301, which houses a Pratt & Whitney 1340. This engine was Pratt & Whitney's first engine. It came out in the 1920s and was the first of the famed Wasp series, It was a single-row, nine-cylinder, air-cooled, radial design and displaced 1,344 cubic inches. It produced 600 horsepower. A total of 34,966 engines were produced before they stopped production in the 1960s.

Air Tractor 301 had a hopper capacity of 320 gallons and had a fuel capacity of 63.3 imperial gallons. Cruise speed was between 120 and 140 miles per hour. Maximum speed of the 301 was 168 miles per hour.

The Air Tractor 401 has a hopper capacity of 400 gallons and a fuel capacity of 105 imperial gallons. It has the same P & W 1340 engine and a longer wing, which makes for shorter field takeoffs. It first flew on September 1979, and certification was awarded in 1980. They are still being produced today. Maximum speed at sea level is 156 miles per hour, with cruise speed between 120 and 140 miles per hour.

P & W also produced Air Tractor 402, 502, 602, and 802. Whenever Air Tractor changed from a 1 to a 2 at the end of their model number, it meant going from an av gas burner to a jet fuel engine.

Thrush Corporation also came out with their 510 and 550 models and their 710. These model numbers also reflect capacity in gallons of the hopper.

The technology that's been added to the ag aviation market over the last twenty to thirty years has been phenomenal. We now have GPS guidance to constant flow control regardless of the ground speed, which we'll talk about a little later. Some of the newer ag planes are now adding airbags built into the seat belts. The Air Tractor 802, which is what I've been flying for the last several years, can carry 800 gallons of water and can produce working speeds of 175 miles per hour or greater. It sports a Pratt & Whitney PT6-65 or 6-67, 1,350 horsepower. It burns anywhere from 75 to 90 gallons of fuel per hour depending on air temperatures. This plane is also used in fire air tanker operations. The price tag for a new 802 will run in the neighborhood of $2 million, equipped with GPS, load hog, flow control, booms, spreader, and single-point fuel.

CHAPTER 3

GPS Systems

Back in the early days, no one had access to GPS systems, and the primary way to work was with either a ground man as a flagger or a device attached to the wing that dispatched a string of tough paper material attached to a cardboard weight. Upon reaching the end of your pass, you could activate a switch in the plane to eject the cardboard, which would then float to the ground, giving you a visual of where your last pass was. The only big drawback with this system was if there was much of a wind, you really didn't know how far your flag floated.

In the high tech world we live in today, pretty much everyone has a GPS of some sort in their planes. In the early days of the GPS systems, most required a pricey annual subscription; most today do not. There are all kinds of models that one can choose from, ranging from about $8,000 upward to as much as $30,000. I run a Satloc G4, which is one of the top of the lines Satloc has today. They all come with some sort of light bar. Some mount these just forward of the hopper door, and I've seen some that mount then inside the cockpit on the dash. Even though these inside light bars are straight forward, they seem a bit odd to me. I want my eyes looking as much outside the cockpit as possible, and when you're trying to follow a light bar mounted on the dash rather than outside, it just seems like a recipe for disaster. For you young pilots that have no idea what the light bar is or how it works, it works like a localizer, and it of course runs off a satellite signal.

The Satloc gives the operator the ability to program the plane's spray width into the computer, which will change with different applications. Most herbicide applications use a narrower swath than a fungicide or insecticide application. Whenever the pilot has to go to dry application, the swath widths will change again as the poundage per acre changes. The higher poundage per acre, the narrower the swath, and of course the lower poundage can be applied at a wider swath.

Whenever a pilot arrives at the field, they should circle the field enough times to pick out any hazards such as a power line, homes, and sensitive plants that they want to stay clear of. After examining the field, the pilot wants to enter with the wind blowing away from his or her pass. This will prevent you from flying back through the chemicals of your past pass. Most modern planes now are equipped with a smoker much like the aerobatic planes use in air shows. As we're spraying, we can click a button that will inject a paraffin-based oil into one of the exhaust pipes. This will produce smoke, which enables the pilot to determine how far the wind is taking the chemical, and if by chance the wind changes directions, the pilot can take corrective action in order to get away from the chemical.

There are several patterns that can be picked inside the Satloc: Back-to-Back, Racetrack, Squeeze, Quick Racetrack. There are several more, but these are the primary ones that I use. My favorite is Racetrack, as your turns never get any wider or shorter. When I'm entering the field on the first pass, I press a button on my flight stick, which will tell the GPS that this is point A. At the end of the first pass, I click it again, and this is point B. After this pass I fly all the way over to the far side of the field and start that pass once again clicking my GPS button, and this tells the GPS that this is point C. After flying this pass, you click it again, and it takes you back to pass number two. Fly pass number two, and at the end of this pass, click it again, and it will guide you to the exact center of the field for your next pass. Just imagine a car on a racetrack making circles with the turns never getting any wider or shorter.

The Squeeze pattern starts with point A, then B, then C, just like in the earlier pattern. Now, however, your passes will continue to get closer together, hence the name Squeeze. The Back-to-Back pattern and the Back-to-Back Skip patterns are just that. Point A, then B, and then it will just take you back to back across the field. Sometimes when I have a very weird-shaped field where nothing is square, I'll use Back-to-Back Skip. It skips a pass every time you advance your GPS button. So you'll have swaths like pass number one, three, five, seven, and so on. After you get to the far side of the field, you hit Setup on your GPS screen and then push the Enter button, and it'll take you back to pass number two, four, six, eight, and so on. One of the advantages of using Back-to-Back Skip is that your turns won't have to be so tight since you are actually skipping a pass with each advance.

Quick Track pattern is where you initiate point A, then point B, and then the pilot guesses as to where the middle of the field is and enters there and advances to point C. Now the plane will fly like the Racetrack pattern. This pattern prevents the pilot from flying from point B all the way over to point C as in the earlier Racetrack or Squeeze patterns. If the field is very wide, this cuts down on the time flying to the far side of the field.

The Racetrack and Quick Track are by far my most favorable patterns to use 90 percent of the time.

The light bar on the Satloc is around fifteen lights wide with three vertical lights in the center. I've always said the light bar is politically correct, as when the lights go left of center, they're red, and when they go right of center, they're green. It's very similar to the OBS head for tracking VORs. If you get off course, you follow the bar, or in the light bar case, you follow the lights. Whenever you get you lights back to the three vertical yellow lights, you are on your correct pass. You can manually set up each light in feet from center and stipulate how far in feet you are in between each light. I have my last bar on either side of center set at three feet. As you can imagine, it doesn't take much rudder to move three feet one way or another while traveling between 140 and 175 miles per hour.

Most light bars also show what swath number you are on, what ground speed you are going, and maybe how many acres you've covered. This all can be preset according to how the pilot wants the number to show up and where. The Satloc also comes with USB ports that allow you to download a job from an office-generated USB drive into your system. When I use the feature, I can then download the job, and my screen inside the cockpit will show the fields on that drive and where they're located in relation to where I am. Whenever I begin to spray or fertilize, it will then begin to "paint" a line across the poly map on my screen, which is really helpful whenever I run out of chemical or fertilizer as I see exactly where to begin spraying or fertilizing upon returning to the field.

After a job or even a day of working, the pilot can then download the jobs selected back onto the USB drive, and it'll produce a product called an "As Applied" map. A paper copy of the job can then be printed to show the farmer how the field was sprayed. We don't have many farmers that require this map, but I know in some parts of the country this is in high demand.

We use a program called ChemMan for our mapping purposes. It comes with a huge database of chemicals, complete with EPA regulation numbers, safety procedures in case of accidents, and the ability to download the current weather after completing the job.

I know there are other good mapping programs out there, such as Ag Sync, and I encourage you to look into each of them and find out what works best for you.

CHAPTER 4

Weather or Not?

Whether you're flying for yourself or for someone else, there'll be times when you'll be biting your nails wondering, *CAN I?* If you're flying for a boss, some, not all, will want you to get the job done regardless of weather. Back in the day when I was studying to become a private pilot, we were taught to remain at least twenty miles from a thunderstorm. As an ag pilot, there have been times when I was pretty much in the middle of the thunderstorm or at least half a mile from it. None by my choosing but more from the pushing of my boss. The most important thing to remember is you're the PIC. If you tear up an airplane, the FAA is not going to be asking your boss why you flew into weather; they're going to be asking you. It's your license and your livelihood on the line, so don't push it.

Several years ago, in what I'm going to share was not one of my brightest days, I got to work one morning with a lot of spraying to get done. The visibility that morning was about fifty feet down the runway. Dense fog had plagued us this morning, and I sat nervously waiting for it to lift. I was flying an older Air Tractor 401, and at that time there was no artificial horizon on the dash. I waited and waited, and it finally began to lift, or so I thought. Just looking down the runway, it appeared that I had at least three-fourths of a mile, maybe more, and it looked like the ceiling had risen to about five hundred feet. All the clearance I needed, at least I thought, so I loaded up the plane with chemical and started rolling down the runway. I lifted off past the point of no return on my short strip and almost immediately flew into a wall of fog with about a twenty-foot ceiling. I immediately turned to the east, hoping I could find some clearing. There was none to be found.

I was barreling across the field adjoining my strip about ten feet off the ground at around 125 miles per hour. I saw a tree line ahead and climbed over it and immediately went back into the fog, so back to the deck I went. By this time, if my heart had had a sound amplifier hooked to it, it beat would've been beating to the tune of the drum solo in the old rock and roll song "Wipeout." All I could do was try and remember what was yet ahead. I was too heavy to try and turn around and land on my short runway, so I was quickly running out of options. Not having any type of attitude indicator or turn-and-ball needle, I knew what was going to happen If I got into the fog for any extended time, but I also knew I was out of options, so I pushed the throttle back to full power and pulled the stick back into my lap.

I immediately flew into the whiteout. I was hoping that I was still wings level as I was climbing through what seemed like three thousand feet of clouds. (I think it was more like three hundred feet, but it seemed like more.) The clouds started getting brilliant white, which was telling me I was getting close to the top. As I popped out on to top of the overcast, I was already in about a thirty-degree bank to the right unbeknownst to me. I then had to fly around for about forty-five minutes for the fog to really dissipate before I could put out the load.

On another day I was flying an Air Tractor 301, and I'd been fertilizing off a municipal airport all day. My ferry times were getting longer and longer as the day went by, so I decided to move to a grass strip closer to my job. I called the owner of the strip and asked permission to use it, which he gave, but not without the warning that it hadn't been mowed in a while and the grass was a bit tall. After talking to him a bit, I decided it would be OK, so off we went. This was a very hot June day with a wind blowing about fifteen miles out of the west, which would've been good, considering I would be taking off into the wind. The runway lay east and west and had a power line at the end running north and south, and behind that was a highway with a very large drainage ditch beyond the highway. It was getting later in the day by the time my fertilizer load truck arrived, and I decided I had to use the wind from the west to my advantage and take off over the wires and other obstructions, "easy peasy." The runway was close to 2,640 feet long, so I thought, *Sure, we can do this*.

Just as I was fixing to take on my first load of this hairy strip, my load truck broke down, so with my plane running, I got out to work on the truck for at least thirty minutes. Finally I got the truck started by standing by the engine and coaxing it. I told my driver not to fully load me this first time till I could see how the plane performed on my first takeoff. After a short time, I assumed that surely I had one-half to three-fourths of a load. Then I walked around to see fertilizer piling up and overflowing out of my hopper.

I immediately screamed at my driver to stop and then proceeded to chastise him about what he had just done. I knew I had only a couple to three options. One was to go to town and find a five-gallon bucket and dip the fertilizer out of the top, which would take forever. The second option was to hit the dump door and drop the fertilizer directly out the bottom, which I really didn't want to do, or the third was to try and fly out of there.

Looking back on the possible accident that was looming that afternoon, I've told several friends over the years that there were several factors that collided that day all at once. While working on the truck and with my plane running, I hadn't noticed that my 15-mile-per-hour headwind had ceased and become a calm wind. The density altitude was extremely high; the grass on the runway was too tall to get any kind of ground speed with a heavy load and all the obstructions at the end. I chose to try the last of the three options.

Upon going full power, the plane began to creep out of its starting point. I was maybe three-quarters of the way down the runway, maybe running around 65 to 70 miles per hour, and the power lines, highway, and large ditch were getting larger and larger in my windshield. To top this off, I was full of avgas. I don't remember thinking of what I did next, which makes me think that this must've been my guardian angel, who's helped me several times. At this point of no return and knowing I couldn't get it stopped before shearing off the landing gear crossing the highway and nose-diving into the big ditch, I applied brakes full on, and the plane immediately went end over. I hit so hard on the top of my cockpit that it broke out, and the ceiling transitioned into a snowplow. By the time I got stopped sliding, the cockpit was full of dirt. I was able to slide out an opening about ten inches wide (still not sure how I did that). I did learn one valuable lesson hanging upside down after the crash, and that was to put my hands above my head before releasing my seat belt. I had survived the crash but about broke my neck falling to the ground.

On another occasion I was working for an operator who did not know the word *stop*. It was go, go, go. I was spraying some milo, and there were thunderstorms less than three miles away approaching fast. I was flying an Air Tractor 502. I had two loads to go and took off with the next to last load. The field was only about two miles west, very close to the thunderstorm. The approaching thunderstorm was gathering intensity and was getting closer to my strip by the seconds. Before I got done with that last load, I was flying in a hard downpour, which didn't really make sense as I was putting out an herbicide. Everyone knows herbicides and hard rains do not like each other, but my boss didn't care. He wanted me to come in and get one more load.

By this time the rain had already reached my grass/dirt runway and had turned into a muddy sloppy mess. The runway was oriented east/west with a small ditch running parallel to the strip and a gravel road on the other side of the ditch. I had a pretty good crosswind from the south. Just as I gently touched down on the runway, the crosswind started pushing me toward the ditch and road. Full right runner wasn't enough, and with no power going over my surfaces and my brakes reminding me of being on ice in my truck, it felt like when you hit your brakes and you swear that you just speeded up, so that was useless. My insistent boss watched as his plane and pilot jumped the ditch and came to a stop in the middle of the gravel road. No injuries this time to the plane or to myself.

Wires and trees are a constant threat. I was beginning to fly a field that I had flown before. My first mistake was not to circle the field and look for hidden obstructions. I thought I knew the field. Unbeknownst to me there was an additional wire lying below the bigger wires, and

I couldn't see it till it was too late. As I was approaching the wires, I made the determination that I could get underneath the bigger wires. As I got closer to them, I discovered another wire hanging about halfway below. If you could enlarge the photo, you'd see the lower wire. It was too late to pull up, so I had to stick to my plan. I caught the lower wire with my vertical and bounced off the ground as I was trying to get under it. I only did minor damage to the plane but did some major nerve damage to my soul.

The main mistake I took away from this incident was not to get in a hurry. Circle the fields and search for any obstructions like lower wires or stray trees. I want to add one more very important comment about go/no go decisions. When approaching wires and you choose to go under or over, don't change your mind at the last second. Stick to your original decision whether right or wrong. It's better to do minor damage to a plane than to end up in the center of some major wires, perhaps totaling the plane and hurting yourself.

All of these stories drive home one of the most important things: You are the pilot in command. It's your decision to go or not to go. This was the case in the three stories I related above: flying in the fog; dealing with the high heat, humidity, and the loss of my headwind plus all the other factors; and finally contending with the boss whose mindset was that it was more important to get this job done so he could invoice it than to do a good job for the customer. I can point my fingers at others all day long, but it ultimately comes down to you and me. Any of these incidents could've taken my life, but I guess my guardian angel is still on the job.

Not everyone is as fortunate as I am. A friend that flew in my area once picked up an odd job down in Alabama spraying trees. He was flying a 502 as well. He and another pilot were trying to move their two planes across a wooded area during some bad weather and very low ceilings. His buddy made it to his destination, but my friend did not. They found him three days later; his plane had literally flown into the tops of some trees. They said it looked like he went in under full power. He'd just lost his visibility, and with no instruments his life was taken from him, his wife, and his children. I don't know if his boss was pushing him to make that trip or if it was solely up to him, but whatever the case, he was responsible.

Never ever let someone make you do something you're not comfortable with, whether your discomfort is due to weather or just lack of experience. Feel good about your job and your task. You'll go home at the end of the day and be with the ones you love.

I've had several friends involved in serious accidents. When flying to a field, very likely between three hundred and five hundred feet, there are two things we pilots look for as we are scanning for other planes:.

1. Seeing a plane above the horizon or...

2. Seeing any left or right movement.

The most dangerous situations of all scenarios is both planes being below the horizon to each other and both heading in opposite directions—in other words, coming straight at each other. In a case like this, you see no movement left or right, and it's very easy to not see each other until it's too late. I had a couple of friends involved in such a scenario: one was taking off in an Air Tractor 502 with a heavy load, and the other pilot that was approaching the same airport empty in an Air Tractor 802, so he was coming in fast in comparison to the 502. They hit head on. The departing 502 pilot saw the 802 pilot at the last second and immediately tried to pull up. This resulted in his right landing gear going through the 802's windshield. They found the 802 pilot's helmet about seventy-five yards away. Here are a few photos. Miraculously they both survived, although the 802 pilot was in and out of the hospital for around a year. Most of the photos are of the 802, and the one photo of the 502 shows the plane back at the airport minus one landing gear.

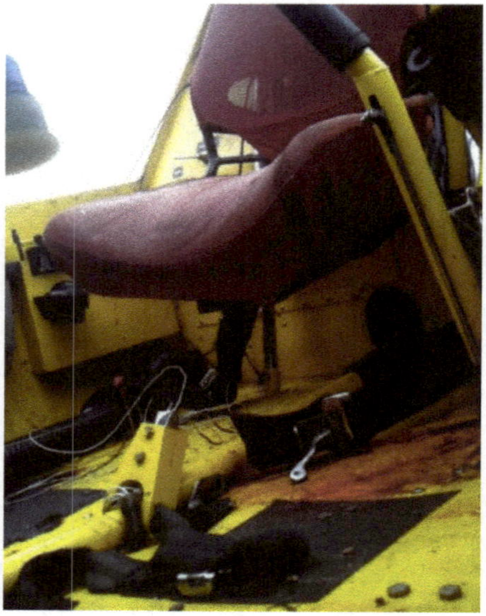

CHAPTER 5

Safety First

I can't overemphasize how important this chapter is because if you're not careful, you might not come home at the end of the day. No matter who your boss is, the safety of you and your plane is up to you and you alone. The pilot can blame the owner all day long for the fitness of the plane, but it all boils down to *the pilot in command*. You and you alone call the shots.

Perform extensive due diligence in making sure your plane is full of oil, enough fuel to perform the job ahead. I've seen several fuel gauges over the years that will lie to you, and it's ended in some embarrassing moments when pilots had to land out in a field because of fuel exhaustion (or air contamination). Know how much fuel your plane burns per hour, then set a timer when you're going to need fuel. Always allow thirty to forty-five minutes reserve as sometimes you'll get in a field that takes way longer to finish than you speculated. The hotter it is, the more fuel and oil you'll consume. You don't want to have to explain to the plane owner why the engine locked up for lack of oil or just plain ran out of gas all because you didn't keep a close eye on it.

Always know your wind and wind speeds and know your plane's limitations. Remember the three *H*s that are killers: High Heat and Humidity. Your plane that leaped off the runway on that cool morning with a big load will act totally different on a high heat and humidity day with the same load. It's always your call as to how big a load you can carry. Don't let your boss or anyone tell you anything different.

When you reach a field, circle that field two or three times and look at all sides, checking for those invisible power lines, poles, pieces of equipment, towers, and such. Look for any homes, swimming pools, fishponds, and traffic, including motorcycles or just someone walking. Know what you're spraying before you leave the ground. Know how harmful it is or isn't to any of the aforementioned. Always begin spraying on the downwind side and work into the wind so as to remain out of your spray from the last pass. It was once thought that the lower you got the better coverage you could get when doing liquid. That's not true. Actually, eight to ten feet is the optimum height for spray products. Fertilizer or cover crop can be applied around treetop high as long as it's not a California Redwood (LOL).

I've been in the ag aviation business for thirty-eight years, and still today I'm always looking for a place to land while working or ferrying. Always keep this in your mind. If you were to lose your engine the first thing to do, if you're able, is to lose your load, then immediately pull back hard on your stick to get to your best glide speed. (You should know this speed from your fight manual.) Doing this will accomplish two things: first, you will have obtained best glide, and second, you will most likely have gained two or three hundred feet, which you may need while executing an emergency descent into a field or road.

Just remember that you may not be able to lose your load if you're over a populated area. You need to get your plane as light as possible and allow the rapid loss of all that weight to help you gain as much altitude as possible. Climb until you reach glide speed, then start searching for a place to land, preferably into the wind. All this may not be possible if you are too low with little load. Just remember what you were taught early on in your flying career. *Keep that plane flying come hell or high water!* Too many pilots are killed each year by stalling and spinning into the ground.

We work and live in a dangerous environment. Treat it as such. Always, always, always, keep in mind the people or animals on the ground and do everything to keep from drifting chemical or fertilizer on them. Too many times I've seen hot dog pilots do some really stupid stuff just to get the job done, relinquishing any thoughts as to the harm they may be causing. It can take a long time to gain a positive attitude from the public concerning our occupation and only a moment to lose that affirmation from said public.

CHAPTER 6

FAA, National and State Associations, and the USDA

Many of you probably already know that you or the company you're flying for will have to obtain a FAR Part 137 Ag Operator Certificate. You have to have this before you can legally begin operations. This means making an appointment with your local FSDO (Flight Standards District Office). They will come to your place of operation. You'll have to do a weight and balance with a load, and then they'll want to see you fly and make an emergency dump of your load. Very important to keep these folks happy because without that certificate, you're out of business. Most inspectors from the FSDO offices will visit two or three times a year to inspect your paperwork and look at the planes to make sure everything still looks airworthy.

Whether your plan looks airworthy can be a matter of opinion. I once hit a turkey buzzard while flying in Kentucky, which left a terrible dent in the leading edge of my right wing. A couple months went by, and we got a visit from a couple of inspectors who didn't say anything about the dent. Then a couple months later, we had two new inspectors show up, and they looked at the dent and grounded my plane as they didn't like the dent. That being said, all inspectors aren't the same. You might get a good one, and you might get one who's trying to make a name for themselves, but I'll have to say most are good and know that we're in the business to help the American farmer be successful.

I feel it's also very important to belong to your state agricultural aviation association along with the National Agricultural Aviation Association (NAAA). The NAAA is based in Washington, DC, and they are the greatest lobbyist for our industry. When you join NAAA, you'll get a great magazine/newspaper chockful of useful stories that you can learn from.

I've spoken of the FAA and the state and national associations, so now I'll talk about the USDA.

The United States Department of Agriculture regulates all applicators, whether they are private or commercial applicators. Before you can become a commercial applicator licensed under the USDA, you have to take a commercial applicators exam and pass with a 70 percent or higher score. You can get the study material from your state's department of agriculture, plant industries division. Tell them you're going to be a commercial agricultural pilot, and they'll send you the study books for a small fee.

There are also other reasons that you might need to deal with the USDA. If you ever have a drift claim and someone makes a phone call to the USDA, you're going to get a visit from your local USDA inspector. The inspector is then going to interview the pilot and go over the spray records that were recorded for that particular claim. If a pilot does end up with a violation, the news piece will get turned in to the local paper, and it won't be your boss whose name will be in the paper; it'll be the pilot's. Plus the pilot will get the monetary fine. Always make sure to follow the chemical label instructions. To avoid getting a violation, know what the wind limit is so you're not flying above that limit. Always know what chemical the ground crew is giving you and how harmful it is to neighboring crops or homes,

With all that being said, being an ag aerial applicator can be a very generous and rewarding occupation—as well as a very dangerous one. I live in southeast Missouri, and our season starts when the temperatures get five to ten degrees above freezing, and the heavy flying ends around September or October. A good ag seat will generate anywhere from $100,000 to $180,000 for those few months of flying.

I would fall short if I didn't add one last chapter about the pilot who guides me, which brings me to my last chapter.

CHAPTER 7

If God Is Your Copilot, Then You're Sitting in the Wrong Seat!

Over thirty-eight years of ag flying and forty-seven years as a pilot, I've experienced some incidents that were unexplainable except to say they had to be divine intervention from my creator.

My first such experience was in my second year in the ag business, when I was flying the C-188 Cessna Ag Truck. This plane had just basic instruments, no radios of any kind, whether business or aviation comms. I'd been working all day out of a small airport that got very little traffic, so I wasn't too concerned about not having a radio. It was probably my twentieth load of the day, and I had just quit looking for other traffic (not a good thing), but I was getting tired, and we pilots get sucked up into the farmer's request of "Hurry up—I needed this done yesterday." Anyway, I was flying back in to get another load and was on about a 1.5 modified left base to my runway when I heard inside my helmet, "Rick, there's a plane."

Without even wondering where this voice had come from, I immediately looked out my right window to see that my plane and a twin who hadn't seen me either were converging and were about to meet in a midair collision. I immediately turned away from him, avoiding the crash. Suddenly it dawned on me that I'd just heard my name called out in warning with no radio of any kind where that could have come from. That totally freaked me out because at this time I was a back-slidden Christian and wasn't living like I should have been.

I've since flown through three wires, and as I mentioned earlier in this book, completely tore a plane up—all due to pilot error. I am a Christian now, and looking back on my career, I can see where God or his angels have intervened on my behalf and got me out of what should've been life-ending situations. I've said often to friends, "When I get to heaven, and if I do get to meet my guardian angel, he's going to tell me, 'I'm glad you're here because I'm tired.'" With all the sophisticated tools we as modern aerial applicators have in our toolboxes, I would be remiss if I didn't mention that we need to lean on God the Father; his son, Jesus; and the Holy Spirit to guide us through every step of the way and add that practice into our toolboxes as well.

Always remember the old saying "There may be old pilots and bold pilots, but there are few old bold pilots."

Happy flying, and please stay safe. You have a family who loves you and wants to see you come home.

Rick McCord
Full Commercial & CFII
573-576-0410

PS: My email address is ricksflying@yahoo.com. Email me anytime with any questions. Also I've teamed up with some insurance companies as a life agent and have been successfully writing life policies for ag pilots to protect their families in the event something tragic happens. Reach out to me anytime.

AGAIN, HAPPY FLYING!

Ingram Content Group UK Ltd.
Milton Keynes UK
UKHW020619120723
424991UK00004B/11